MEDITATING
CAT

Day Breaks
on the Bottom of a
Blue Sea

Poems

David Oliver Cranmer

© 2025 by David Cranmer

All rights reserved.

No part of this book may be reproduced in any form or by any means without the prior written consent of the publisher, except where permitted by law.

Cover image from Adobe Stock. Cover design and interior line drawings by dMix.

ISBN: 978-1-943035-37-3

Meditating Cat
Imprint of BTAP

The poems "Woebegone, Far Away" and "Watching Bad Day at Black Rock" are homages to the film *Bad Day at Black Rock* (1955), screenplay by Millard Kaufman and Don McGuire, an adaptation of a Howard Breslin short story.

For Denise Marie & Ava Elyse, my charmers.

SANDPIPER

I run along life's shore
dodging the cold spray
of those surfing
the same waves
of past slights,
real and reimagined,
until the storms
transform into tsunamis

These champion surfers
are charged by the
surge of drama,
never growing weary, and
I've become an accomplished
long-distance runner,
avoiding their heavy, wet sand
in my shoes.

From David Oliver Cranmer's debut poetry collection ...

Cranmer's debut chapbook reflects on loss, "canceled" icons, crimes of passion, and cold-blooded murder. He probes the breaking point of inner spirit and navigates the deep streams of depression, eventually lifting the veil of despair to reveal glimmers of sanguinity, holding to the belief that "each day breaks with such hope."

Table of Contents

Twilight Falls and the Monsters Are Due	1
Woebegone, Far Away	2
Watching Bad Day at Black Rock	3
The Crow's Cap	4
The Tree Stand	5
Study Suggests Sleeping Spiders Dream	7
Limelight	8
Charity Checkout	9
I Just Saw Him Last Tuesday	10
Birch to Maple	12
On the Walk (haikus)	15
John Prine Didn't Have to Die	32
At the Hotel Bar, To My Left	33
The Downhill Racer	34
Mmm, Naan	38
Goliath	39
Not a Sunflower, Maybe a Bleeding Heart	40
On the Bottom of a Blue Sea	41
Her Reflections	42
Contentment	43
Day Breaks	44

About the Poems

These schematic, free verse, and haiku revelations were written over a seven-year period from 2017 through 2024, though memories stretch back down a fifty-year road. Seasons come and go and try as I may to create some sequential cohesion, these verses demanded to be presented out of order for thematic reasons all their own.

Day Breaks at the Bottom of a Blue Sea

Don't be afraid to suffer—take your heaviness
and give it back to the earth's own weight;
the mountains are heavy, the oceans are heavy.

Rainer Maria Rilke
from *Sonnets to Orpheus*

Twilight Falls and the Monsters Are Due

The unbidden lurks,
as anxiety mounts
over life's frailty
—setting off a burst of barks
that fails to beat it back.

The seed is sewn,
the weight takes root.
Even my girl playing
"Chopsticks" as a lark,
can't change the weather.

I don't scream into the wind,
or whine, blaming the universe.
I take it in, absorb the blows—
mercy will come
by daybreak

Woebegone, Far Away

Iron horse on desert rails,
—and blown out human shell.
Regrets drag this life across

technicolor wastelands.
Nothing but big empty,
woebegone and far away.

The past like driven nails,
pierce unguarded souls,
we are only as big as

what we seek but the price
paid for those returns are,
woebegone and far away.

Watching Bad Day at Black Rock

Dust will settle (you see)
I pushed to make troublesome
go away but pushed too fast,

too hard and the shrapnel
damaged not just me but a
close friend I cared deeply for

(You see) "It's a small world …
but such an unfriendly one,"
so, let's watch Spencer Tracy

amend what's been broken,
clean up the town, clear away
the webs, and never look back.

The Crow's Cap

A black, flat cap
came home to roost
after many years
of trying,
the cap hadn't changed,
I did, what with my
grey beard & crow's feet—
we are now inseparable

The Tree Stand

The sun was breaking through the wooded canopy,
yet it was bitter in the shade of the trees,
a dusting of snow had fallen the night before.

I slouched in my father's tree stand, shivering.
I had begged him to take me hunting,
and he had finally relented.

"Why did you build the fort here?"

Dad smiled, "This is a tree stand, not a fort."

"Why did you build the tree stand here?"

"The well-worn path you see at the base of the tree, that's where the deer wander past, on their way to Fall Creek."

"Why is the tree stand so high up?"

"We don't want the deer to see or smell us, do we?"

"No, I guess not," I said.

I loved spending time with my dad
—not so much the hunting, I
would never kill a deer, that's not me.
It was being allowed into the grown-up world,
a sneak peek or coming attractions, if you will,
of the future.

I gazed at a can of Old Milwaukee in his hand.
He caught me looking and asked me if I was thirsty.
My eyes widened, I nodded with a grin.

"Just a sip. Don't tell your mother," he said.

Dad handed me the can, and I swallowed a taste.

Lips twisted, I grumbled, "That's awful!"

He laughed, patted me on the back and took the can.

"Dave," it was the first time I remember him
calling me that, not David, "we need to be
quiet now and wait."

I placed a finger in the snow on the edge of the stand
and ran it along the side, watching the flurries cascade
to the ground, waiting in silence with my father.
We didn't see a deer at all that day, though
I now know it was the bond
we strengthened that mattered.

Study Suggests Jumping Spiders Dream

What gifts does the Sandman bring
to the tiny arachnid that has drifted off,
all four pairs of eyes in REM?
The study didn't hypothesize.

Perchance—

An endless supply of flies on a stick
like carnival treats?
Silken tents large enough for all
hundred spiderlings to stay at home? Or

Nightmares!

Tangled in its own dragline, watching a
ravenous centipede close in for the kill,
or a ginormous shoe coming down
at lightning speed.

Limelight

Thank you for sitting with me
in the limelight
of a Charleston, West Virginia, hotel
that's seen better days.
The white-hot light is dimming
and we both know where this is going
but thanks for playing along
you saying it's going to be alright.

Charity Checkout

Pumping gas at $4.00 a gallon
and the thermometer is dropping,
the weight of snow is in the air.

A woman passes wearing
a thin, black coat with large daisy print
hood up, tied tight around her face
her bare ankles exposed in summer capris—

into the convenience store,
I grab a newspaper and lottery ticket,
at what point did rounding up
at checkout clear my conscience?
admittedly, it did

I Just Saw Him Last Tuesday

"I think Carl's dead," Pete said.

Many years removed, I still remember the shaken disbelief of Carl's friend as
we walked down the gravel drive from my home to the cottage that Carl rented from me.
I stepped in while Pete waited outside for the coroner.

The death stench was palpable in the small, three-room space.
It took less than twenty steps from the entrance to get to the bedroom where he lay, contorted.

In his day, Carl was a tough-as-nails bouncer at Tweitman's Halfway House,
kicking ass long before age dictated him a paint-slinger, then quiet retirement.
And now—

His legs hung sprawled off the side of the bed, in tighty-whities,
his left ball sack hanging out, and his tongue drooped out of the side of his mouth.

Death was not kind to Carl.
Or, as I prefer to imagine—the old bouncer gave it one hell of a final tussle.

I pulled a blanket over him and joined Pete outside.

"I just saw him last Tuesday," he said, still shaking his head in disbelief.
I only nodded, words suppressed by the jarring sight of death outside of a funeral home's softening hands.

"Just last Tuesday," Pete repeated.

Timor mortis conturbat me.

Birch to Maple

my hand glides
over hickory bark,
smooth maple and
papery birch,
tangible needs, I feel,
root my emotions,
nature's comfort
for a time out of joint
even when things
are not okay,
it's going to be okay

All truly great thoughts are conceived by walking.

Friedrich Nietzsche

On the Walk

on the walk
trilliums and violets
our early spring blooms

spring brook roars,
like me,
carving new beginnings

jazz patter
on maple leaves
dewy kisses

old, tired limbs sway and
groan by the creek while strolling
on the rocky bank

my heart, like a leaf
dropped into the creek, follows
the currents away

creative crossroads,
pushing off into the stream,
far past the shallows

The ocean tides obey the pull of the moon
As a vessel of half water with a pinch of salt
How much of me is affected by the moon's gentle tug?

grey skies
opened up
to a still soul

history's tide   crashes on shore
sounds of conch shells   nothing more

nature's poetry
humbles, rendering my words
insignificant

still

I write tirelessly,
like bees to pollen,
words gathered and stored
to upload to the hive

sadness swirls within
cotton candy-colored clouds
smiles are welcomed here

crisscrossed
an old friend
on a rocky path

ahead loveliness,
she breaks away, graces me
briefly, then flies on

mourning doves
serenading
on the sun-drenched path (after Basho)

thunder rumbles and
I go inside as she stays
out, it's where we part

Her. Me. Alike, and
unlike, but flush with respect
and love countersunk (for d)

let me know
where you are at,
life is moving fast

a lone black-capped soul
observing my movements with
greatest interest

ruby, my dear
flitting bloom to bloom—
balancing nature

on meditation mat
all eyes on me,
house spider

offset curtains
divide the rising sun
from our sleepy room

ornamental smile—
she said it may be time
to turn down her sunshine

scraping life's rust
down to the mettle

from any 'ole window,
I spot death all-around as
God intended life

hawk's shadow across
garden, I glance up, and see
a mouse 'hang gliding'

lament—
swatted, killed a sweat bee
not a mosquito

memory's palette
awash in color where concrete
reality dies

we're living bridges
to loved ones passed on, stewards
of their memories

I think of Larkin dead
and how terrified he'd be
if he only knew

surname origin—
'cranes' dipping their long
bills in the picturesque 'meres'

black dog on a chain
contained by a tiny pill—
but Goodfellow's bored

diamondbacks
slither peacefully
among the doe eyed

the road to
milk & honey—
blemished by war

bee,
hidden on a grape—
my lip swells

we are the mold
on the rind of a bountiful orange
sucking the fruit dry

holdin' angst in the
golden rye fields, catching
kids too close to the cliffs

lovely stars
date night—
broke down on roadside

mantis in amber
12 million years of silent
quarter, Praying still

order is found   in changing seasons
like your smile   by my side

autumn trees   overgrown trails
lead to contentment   enchantment

autumn's weathered kiss   shaking
releasing still art   at our feet

Aeolus
shuffles
brittle, brown leaves
back and forth

autumn twilight—
life screened in
sepulchral tones

in white winter cap
Jack says goodbye to autumn
with an icy stare

lost in a haven
of words; even odd semi-
colons can hang out

anger became currency,
sighs poured out like water—
I drew meditation's bowstring

fingers
struggling with the uke,
winter joints

raven
on sumac
shaking off snow

a moving picture
with no last act, just
a suitcase of poems,
to Avalon he slides

finally,
following lifetime anxiety,
a meditating cat

John Prine Didn't Have to Die

Hotel bathroom ceiling peeling,
white paint twisting and curling
like the bark on a birch tree,
imperiling its pith deeper down

up from my morning constitutional,
knee buckling, a ligament snapping,
like an overladen tree branch, dry,
the obvious plays in mind
—everything decays when old

Though Prine didn't have to die
that April day,
the septuagenarian still in his creative prime,
shuffled off from a goddamn viral load
too high, and too new

At the Hotel Bar, To My Left

Authenticity with ink,
"Be ye wise as serpents,
harmless as doves"

served with a smile
in form-fitted Olivia Rodrigo,
tongue-out, T-shirt

Warhol and the Stones,
Simmons with KISS, Miley too,
like so many in pop culture

but seems
Albert got there
first in '51, right?

unless, lol,
an alabaster disk of Enheduanna
tongue out is dug up in old Ur—

strange it would be to stick
my tongue out right now and go
"bleh!"

what would Authenticity think?

The Downhill Racer

As a kid, I loved winters in upstate New York, especially on weekday mornings after a big snowstorm. I would wake up early to listen to the school closings on the radio, and as soon as it was announced I was off for the day, I would rush outside to go sledding on the gravel driveway that sloped down from the quiet country road where my family lived. I had to be quick before Dad had a chance to scatter rock salt. That sodium-chloride mixture spelled disaster for my snowy runway—the small pockets of exposed dirt and stones steadily grew into large islands as the sun peeked out, eventually ruining my day of fun.

On the weekends my dad would humor me, but not on a work day. Even a light covering of packed snow made the incline a slippery challenge for my old man's Chevy Silverado. He'd feather the truck's accelerator just the right amount, gradually gaining momentum until he reached the top. He had developed as much skill creeping up the hill as I did gliding to the bottom. When my mom was behind the wheel, it was a calamity. She'd always gun it, spinning the tires, going nowhere. I can still see my dad running toward the truck time and again, wildly flailing his hands and yelling for her to "Ease off!" Looking back now, I'm sure she did it for kicks more than anything else.

My adventures as a downhill racer didn't begin on a sled. My father, who'd been a youngster during the Great Depression, mused over how children from poor families in those times used shovels as makeshift sleds. Because life has a way of coming around full circle and in the early 1980s the country was in a recession, my parents didn't have the money to buy the sleek, shiny runner sled that I had seen at the store. So, there I was, sitting on a shovel blade, holding onto the handle stretched out in front of me. My first couple of takeoffs were awkward, but soon enough my skills developed with the unwieldy digging tool.

The year I turned twelve, my mom watched in horror as I zipped down a sheet of ice and our Alaskan malamute, Tooka, bounded straight into my path— there was no way to avoid a crash. In a tangle of legs, paws, and arms, we went yelping across the slick surface and into a snowbank. Luckily no bones were broken, but, in a nod to safety, that Christmas my parents scraped together the money for the sled I'd been eyeing at the store.

My new-fangled runner sled proved easy to adjust to. I'd take it to the top of the slope, and then sprint at full speed before jumping aboard, flat on my stomach. Eventually, I discovered how to throw my weight to the side and deftly balance the sled on one runner, which turned out handy navigating the narrow passages of melting snow and ice. Now and then, my sister Meta would bring out her toboggan and challenge me to a race. But her toboggan was no match for my runner sled. I'd take the lead and zoom far ahead until she had vanished from sight behind me.

Close calls still happened from time to time. Once, I was at the top of the hill and didn't see when family friends who'd come to visit with my parents were backing their car out of the driveway. Panic struck when I realized the driver hadn't seen me bulleting down the hill, heading straight for a collision. I quickly mustered some intestinal fortitude (a locution my dad often said) and using my one-runner trick, I managed to tilt the sled up on its right side, barely squeezing between the car and the edge of the driveway. But the left sled handle nicked the car's back bumper which sent me careening into the ditch. The car stopped with everyone jumping out to come and check on me. Even Tooka came springing across the snow-covered yard to my side, and in a Rockwellian winter scene, she licked my face seemingly to ask if I was okay. I was shaken but not discouraged, and the scare didn't stop me from getting back up on my sled mere minutes after our visitors left.

    For several years after, winter snows brought the same routine—minus any car incidents—with just as much fun and thrills … that is, until other teenage interests like music and girls took hold. Over the passing seasons the metal runners rusted, and the sled became buried deep in the garage. I suspect my dad took it to the landfill or, hopefully, found it a new home for another kid from the neighborhood to enjoy.

    Now I'm forty-five years old, and memories flood back as I take my four-year-old daughter Ava sledding at the community park where parents and kids gather. This hill is much wider, longer, and steeper than my little slope of yesteryear. Gone are the old-fashioned toboggans and steel-and-wood sleds, replaced with plastic saucers and boogie boards. Still, the bigger pleasure is to see families reveling in outdoor activities together. Another cycle is complete.

As I glance over at the older kids a little farther away on a sharper incline, I see to their credit a couple of racers in the mix. It reminds me of a quote from Gertrude Stein that goes, "It is the soothing thing about history that it does repeat itself." A thin smile works its way across my face. Though they have youth on their side, I know I could give any one of them a run for their money … if only I had my old runner sled.

Mmm, Naan

Kneading dough
I sift through
quirky thoughts
on food and death,

musing how we eat the living
in order to survive.
Even if we consumed dirt
we'd still be eating
living microbes
among the sandy grains.

The yeast was happy
in the warm, sugar-water bath
until 'killed'—
smothered in flour then
fried on a hot pan.

Oh, to be an autotroph!

Goliath

Inside a matchbox
with a rock for a headstone
lies our Goliath

a tiny triops
who measured great joy for his
aquatic be-bops

Not a Sunflower, Maybe a Bleeding Heart

When I'm gone
paint a picture for me
or write a few haikus.
Listen to your favorite songs
and if you are taking requests,
some jazz will do.
Pick a sunflower
or better yet
just admire it,
let it live and die
like I did, then
when you walk past
it'll cross your mind:
(knowing me as you do)
he'd probably be complaining
that he would've been happier
as a bleeding heart
in the shade.

On the Bottom of a Blue Sea

My daughter Ava sees
a crane fly adrift in a blue pool of
melted 'bayberry and currant' wax,
and shouts out, "We need to save it!"
But clearly its destiny has been met.

We decide that the crane fly
might been drawn to the well of
pleasant aromatics and soft glow
of the plug-in scent warmer
because it wanted a spa day.
We turn off the light.

Later, we find its thin body
frozen in a waxy tomb.
We'll take the hardened blue brick
and bury the crane fly in the backyard
—because it helps my little one deal
with the death of the littlest things.

Her Reflections

She pulls her new blue sundress
over her frame and immediately
bemoans, "The hemline is too short,"

To which I say, "it's okay."
She angles back and forth in the mirror
laments, "I wish I had a butt,"

To which I reply, "it's fine."
She turns to the side, straightens her back, and
regrets, "I need to stop slouching,"

To which I go, "we both do."
She pivots some more, and I can tell from
years of watching, she'll keep the dress.

Contentment

Afternoon—
Sublime food
Thoughtful books
Clearest sky
Cool blue pool
Roaring laughs
Feeling good
—Do not move!

Day Breaks

A verse or two
May strip another's burden.
Tiny blocks of language
Carefully arranged to lessen
Grieving, distress, and tears.

So here I am
Treading the deep,
To fasten a lifeline of buoys
Just for you, yeah you up there,
        Remember
"Each day breaks with such hope."

Previously Published Poems

Limelight
Twilight Falls and the Monsters Are Due
—*Punk Noir Magazine*, 5/12/2022

Woebegone, Far Away
—*Outcast Press*, Autumn/Winter issue, 12/22/2022

John Prine Didn't Have to Die
—*Punk Noir Magazine*, 12/1/2023

Three haikus:
. the road to
. a moving picture
—*Punk Noir Magazine*, 8/22/2023

About the Author

David Oliver Cranmer's poems, short stories, articles, and essays have appeared in *Live Nude Poems*, *Needle: A Magazine of Noir*, *The Five-Two: Crime Poetry Weekly*, *LitReactor*, *Punk Noir Magazine*, Macmillan's *Criminal Element*, and *Chicken Soup for the Soul*. He's learning late in life the benefits of meditation and has discovered he is capable of playing an instrument after failing to make headway with the piano, harmonica, and ocarina. He spends as much time as possible enjoying the outdoors in scenic upstate New York with his family and two cats.

MEDITATING
CAT

www.ingramcontent.com/pod-product-compliance
Lightning Source LLC
Chambersburg PA
CBHW020022050426
42450CB00005B/592